'70s Sausages

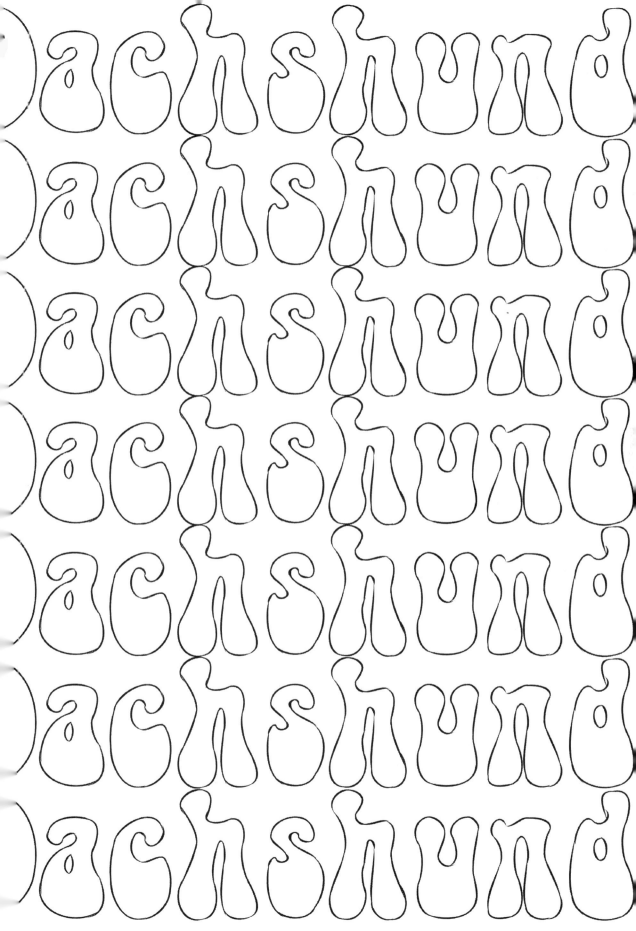

G SAUSAGE DOG

AUSAGE DOG SA

G SAUSAGE DOG

AUSAGE DOG SA

G SAUSAGE DOG

AUSAGE DOG SA

G SAUSAGE DOG

AUSAGE DOG SA

G SAUSAGE DOG

AUSAGE DOG SA

'70s Sausages

Published 2021.
©2021 Gemma Robinson.

ISBN   979 8 72445 874 0

All rights reserved. No part of this publication
may be reproduced without written permission.

Designed and edited by Gemma Robinson.

Printed in Great Britain
by Amazon